HOW SHOULD WE
PRAY AT PRAYER
MEETINGS?

✕ CULTIVATING BIBLICAL GODLINESS

Series Editors

Joel R. Beeke and Ryan M. McGraw

Dr. D. Martyn Lloyd-Jones once said that what the church needs to do most of all is "to begin herself to live the Christian life. If she did that, men and women would be crowding into our buildings. They would say, 'What is the secret of this?'" As Christians, one of our greatest needs is for the Spirit of God to cultivate biblical godliness in us in order to put the beauty of Christ on display through us, all to the glory of the triune God. With this goal in mind, this series of booklets treats matters vital to Christian experience at a basic level. Each booklet addresses a specific question in order to inform the mind, warm the affections, and transform the whole person by the Spirit's grace, so that the church may adorn the doctrine of God our Savior in all things.

HOW SHOULD WE
PRAY AT PRAYER MEETINGS?

RYAN M. MCGRAW

REFORMATION HERITAGE BOOKS
GRAND RAPIDS, MICHIGAN

Reformation Heritage Books
3070 29th St. SE
Grand Rapids, MI 49512
616-977-0889
orders@heritagebooks.org
www.heritagebooks.org

Printed in the United States of America
23 24 25 26 27 28/10 9 8 7 6 5 4 3 2

ISBN 978-1-60178-505-3

For additional Reformed literature, request a free book list from Reformation Heritage Books at the above regular or e-mail address.

HOW SHOULD WE
PRAY AT PRAYER
MEETINGS?

———— ✘ ————

Prayer meetings are a vital aspect to the life and ministry of the church.[1] Yet various challenges arise in relation to prayer meetings. Many people do not prioritize corporate prayer because they do not understand the importance attached to prayer meetings in Scripture.[2] Others attend prayer meetings and lose sight of the kingdom-centered focus that should characterize these meetings. In addition, prayer meetings can be difficult to manage by those leading them. While Christians often go to prayer directly in private, this is rarely the case when they pray in large groups. When churches gather for corporate prayer, instead of focusing on prayer primarily, they often spend much of the time taking prayer requests

---

1. This booklet is extensively revised and expanded from Ryan M. McGraw, "How to Pray at Prayer Meetings," *Ordained Servant*, 2014. Used with permission.

2. Ryan M. McGraw, *How Do Preaching and Corporate Prayer Work Together?*, Cultivating Biblical Godliness (Grand Rapids: Reformation Heritage, 2014).

or conducting Bible studies. Prayer can be virtually sidelined as though it were an afterthought, in which fellowship meals, teaching, or updates on current events in the congregation dominate the time.

Knowing how to pray at prayer meetings can help both those who lead prayer meetings and those who participate in them make prayer meetings more fruitful in relation to their intended purposes. The best way to know how we should pray at prayer meetings and how to lead prayer meetings is to remember the goals that should characterize prayer meetings. The primary purpose of prayer meetings should be to promote the Father's glory through spreading the kingdom of His Son, doing His will by the Spirit's power.

This booklet presents ways to foster proper participation in prayer meetings. The directions below highlight some common pitfalls to avoid in corporate prayer, along with their remedies. Most of these points respect our relationship in prayer to others present at the meeting as well as how best to use our time when we meet for prayer. All who attend prayer meetings should participate actively in prayer, either by praying themselves, by saying their "amens" to the prayers of others (1 Cor. 14:16), or by doing both.

The following directions are suggestive only, and many of them lack the full force of "thus saith the Lord." The goal of this material is to improve our prayer meetings as effective means of advancing the gospel and of edifying the saints by drawing on general principles from Scripture, Christian experience, and sanctified common sense.

PRIORITIZE THE FIRST THREE PETITIONS OF THE LORD'S PRAYER

The primary purpose of prayer meetings should be to spread the glory of God through gospel preaching and personal evangelism. The coming of God's kingdom and the doing of His will are the two primary means by which He spreads His glory throughout the world. Our prayer meetings should reflect the fact that the Father is seeking people who will worship Him in Spirit and in truth (John 4:21–24). At the prayer meeting, pray for the Father to glorify Himself through spreading the gospel of His Son. Pray that the Spirit would spread the kingdom through blessing the preaching of the word, especially on the Lord's Day.

This does not mean that we should not pray for the needs of the church more generally. It means that we should pray for one another with the goal of spreading God's glory through honoring His name, furthering His kingdom, and doing His will. This means that praying for the conversion of unconverted people, the work of missionaries, church planters, and theological seminaries, as well as for the evangelistic efforts of our own and other denominations should dominate the content of our prayer meetings.

Prioritizing the first three petitions of the Lord's Prayer in corporate prayer makes our prayers more catholic in tone. This means that our prayers express an overarching concern for the spread of God's glory universally through the Spirit's work in the church in every part of the world. Private prayer is a better context for expressing private concerns than corporate prayer is. Public prayer should generalize our prayers in light of those things that concern all believers deeply. God's honor, His kingdom, and His will should be the bright center of our prayer meetings, radiating into and illuminating all of our prayers.

PRAY FOR OTHER THINGS IN LIGHT OF THE FIRST THREE PETITIONS OF THE LORD'S PRAYER

This is related to the previous point, but it takes us one step further in our prayer meetings. We all have many needs, and every Christian faces his or her own trials. We must avoid both extremes of allowing such immediate needs to dominate our attention in public prayer on the one hand and ignoring them entirely on the other. Letting the first three petitions of the Lord's Prayer provide the context for our prayers for our daily needs, the forgiveness of our sins, and our ability to persevere through personal trials helps retain the kingdom-centered focus of our prayer meetings without neglecting the communion of the saints. The rule of the kingdom must always be that we should seek first God's kingdom and His righteousness, trusting that He will add all other things to us (Matt. 6:33).

Praying for people's needs in light of the first three petitions of the Lord's Prayer will transform how we pray for them. For example, we should pray for the sick so that they might know Christ better through their illnesses or come to know Him under them. We should pray that the sick would recover, but we must remember that this is a secondary end in praying for them. Applying such kingdom-focused prayers to all physical needs and outward trials is the best way to promote the God-centered emphasis that should mark public prayer. They are also the best means of helping believers and unbelievers alike through our prayers.

When we pray for external needs, we should avoid turning prayer meetings into gossip sessions. Those present at the prayer meeting are usually less abreast of the private details of the lives of many of the people for whom we pray than those bringing such requests are. The rest of us rarely need the level of detail that people are willing to provide when making prayer requests. Do not give too much detail about those for whom we pray, either by way of requests or in your prayers. The Lord knows our needs and those of others better than we know them ourselves. He will always bless our prayers for the growth of the saints in the midst of affliction. We have the assurance that when we ask anything according to His will, He hears us (1 John 5:14). Our sanctification and that of others is His will (1 Thess. 4:3). He will use some of our prayers for the conversion of the lost in their affliction as well (1 Tim. 2:1–3). Praying with the right ends in view curtails our tendency to gossip in offering requests on behalf of others by generalizing the details that we need in order to pray for them.

This does not imply that we should not pray for physical needs in our prayer meetings. Neither does it mean that the bulk of prayer requests will not revolve around physical needs or circumstances in life. There are only so many ways in which we can ask others to pray for God's glory, the spread of His kingdom, and the doing of His will. Someone is always sick and suffering inside the church and out of it on this side of glory. The principle of praying for the last three petitions of the Lord's Prayer in light of the first three petitions can keep our prayer meetings on track. It makes us remember why we are praying in the first place.

PRAY SCRIPTURE

Praying using scriptural language and content is the best way to be assured that God will answer our prayers and that we will gain the consent of others in the prayer meeting. Fewer people will disagree with the Scriptures themselves in corporate prayer than will disagree with personal opinions about family, politics, and current events. If people attending the prayer meetings do not consent to Scripture, then they face deeper problems. Using Scripture in prayer promotes a catholic spirit in prayer in which all believers present can participate gladly.

Praying Scripture is the best means of honoring God and of edifying believers. This does not mean parroting Scripture citations back to God, but thoughtfully using and applying scriptural language and ideas in our prayers. Doing so will improve your private prayers as well. Jonah's mind and heart were so filled with Scripture that his prayer from the belly of the fish in Jonah 2 echoed many parts of the Old Testament. We must learn to think and to speak in biblical language.

One helpful way to do this is to use the Psalms as models for our public and private prayers. Psalms enable us to vent our desires before the Lord in virtually any situation in which we find ourselves. They provide sanctified channels through which to pour out our hearts to the God who is our refuge (Ps. 62:8). We can also draw biblical language and truths from recent sermons in order to help us pray in biblical terms. This practice will reinforce the sermons we hear and enable us to grow in our knowledge of Scripture though practical use. Praying Scripture unites believers in prayer more readily than any other means of praying.

COME IN ORDER TO PRAY

Do not spend too much time on prayer requests. We gather to pray at prayer meetings, not to be updated on the latest news. Use prayer chains, email lists, or smaller groups to share minute details and minor requests. Do not give minute-by-minute updates on the state of the sick. I have seen some people do this every time the church gathers to pray. After the second time, the rest of the group has already begun to realize that they have nothing new to report.

Come to pray for the lost rather than to talk about them. Do not enumerate the names of every lost family member and neighbor. The Lord knows our needs and theirs. Every Christian present has unconverted family members, friends, and neighbors who lay heavy on their hearts. We cannot list them all every week, but the Lord can hear our prayers for them all even when we do not name them one by one.

Corporate prayer should prioritize corporate needs and requests. Use the Psalms as a model in this regard. The prayers contained in the Psalms transcend time, and they rarely include specific names or circumstances. When they do, these are usually relegated to the titles of individual psalms. We should not need lengthy requests to help us pray with understanding as a church. Use other means and occasions for these purposes.

Remembering that we are gathered to pray should affect how we approach Bible studies accompanying prayer meetings as well. A short Bible study can help prepare people to participate in prayer meetings. However, long Bible studies can crowd out prayer. The purpose of the meeting is prayer rather than Bible study. Corporate prayer makes

Bible studies and preaching effective through seeking the power of the Holy Spirit on both. People need to know that prayer is the main event at the prayer meeting and that prayer is vital even if there is no study (or meal) attached to it. While Bible studies and meals are good things, anything that detracts from spending most of the time in corporate prayer distorts the nature of the prayer meeting, transforming it into something else.

DO NOT BE TOO SPECIFIC IN CORPORATE PRAYER

Everyone in a prayer meeting winces inwardly when someone prays in vivid detail about things like the latest fight in their household—everyone, apparently, except those offering such inappropriate prayers. Respect the private details of people's lives in prayer meetings. Those who are present do not need to know most of the details of most of the petitions that we bring in order to join with us in prayer.

We can sometimes act superstitiously when we assume that we need a list of names for which to pray that includes every individual who concerns us. Being specific is important in private prayer, but being too specific can become distracting in public prayer. The Lord knows the names of those who are on our hearts. He can hear corporate prayer for lost people and other needs whether or not others know all of these names.

This does not mean that we should never pray for people by name, but we must be sparing in doing so. It is more profitable to do so only when specific names add to the substance of the prayer meeting and promote the efficacy of our prayers together. Praying for expectant mothers and those recently committed to hospitals can be a great encouragement that tightens the bonds of fellowship among the saints. Yet trying to list the needs of everyone that the group knows becomes both time-consuming and tedious.

Turning prayer into a commentary on current events, whether personal or public, transforms prayer meetings into gossip sessions. This happens more frequently than most people realize. Giving personal details on people's lives when it is not necessary to do so does not cease to be gossip because we baptize it under the guise of a prayer request.

PRAY SO THAT OTHERS CAN SAY "AMEN"

One of our goals in praying at prayer meetings should be to pray in a way that enables our fellow believers to unite with us in prayer and to say their "amens" to the prayers we offer (1 Cor. 14:16). The Bible expects us to say "amen" in corporate prayer. This is the briefest and perhaps the most ancient confession of faith in Scripture. As the Westminster Shorter Catechism notes, in our "amen," we testify "our desire and assurance to be heard" (Q. 107). We should say "amen" at the close of those prayers that we agree with to show that we have adopted them as our prayers. We should pray in a way that others in the room can say "amen" to our prayers as well by making them their own.

We cannot say "amen" to someone's prayer unless we both understand and agree with what is prayed. Those who pray in corporate prayer meetings are speaking for every Christian present at the meeting. In this respect, it is helpful to avoid using "I" in prayer meetings. Using "we" in prayer is a good indicator of whether our petitions and praises are appropriate to the prayer meeting. If you cannot preface your requests or adoration with "we," then your prayer is likely not fitting for public use.

We should avoid personal confession of sin in corporate prayer. Daniel, Ezra, and others confessed sins in public prayer that they could confess with the congregation. When you confess personal instead of corporate sins in the prayer meeting, you put your brothers and sisters in an awkward position as they pray with you. When they say "amen," then this comes across as expressing agreement that you are such a great sinner who needs repentance and forgiveness. While this may be true, it does not set the right tone for prayers in which many hearts are joined.

Avoid polemical issues in corporate prayer as much as possible. For example, if you are a Presbyterian who is praying in a Baptist prayer meeting, then do not pray for the Lord's blessing on household baptisms as a divine ordinance. Polemics are utterly inappropriate in corporate prayer. They are repulsive in this context, even though they are necessary in other settings. When we practice household baptisms in a Presbyterian church, then we should pray for the ordinance whether or not everyone present agrees with it. However, praying for the spread of the kingdom and the glory of God through Christ by the Spirit is something that all Christians can and should unite over across confessional lines.

We are most ecumenical when we join our hearts in corporate prayer. We should express this fact both by saying "amen" audibly in response to the prayers of others and by praying in a way that enables others to adopt our prayers as their own.

AVOID POLITICAL REFERENCES IN YOUR PRAYERS

We must pray for rulers and for all who are in authority that they might come to the knowledge of the truth and that they might allow us to lead quiet and peaceable lives in holiness and reverence (1 Tim. 2:1–2). We should pray that they would enact just laws, punish the wicked, and reward the upright (Rom. 13:1–7; 1 Peter 2:14).

However, prayer meetings are not the time to sort out our differences over which presidential candidate to vote for or what laws to pass. Therefore, we should avoid mentioning things such as bills and referendums by name in our public prayers. Why should we need to? Does not God know better than we do how to direct our governing authorities? Your ideas of just laws and wars may not be the same as the Lord's. You may hold your opinions on such things, but you should also learn to exercise humility among fellow Christians in relation to them, especially in corporate prayer.

We should pray in light of the ethical principles set forth in Scripture rather than in light of those laws that we think promote these principles best. How many wars have been fought where both sides thought their cause was just? We cannot see things as God sees them. Our perspectives are far too limited. We often think that we can pray more accurately on national and international matters than is actually the case. If everyone in the prayer meeting got what they asked for in relation to politics, this would likely lead any nation into catastrophic disorder.

Leave the specifics in political matters to your closet. Pray corporately in a way that is truly corporate. Even if your position is right, corporate prayer is the wrong context in which to express it. Corporate prayer assumes agreement among those who pray; it is neither the place nor the time to pick political battles. If we pray for all other petitions in light of the first three petitions of the Lord's Prayer, then this will lead us to pray for our rulers and for nations more appropriately.

AVOID VAIN REPETITION

It is easier to fall into vain repetition (Matt. 6:7) in prayer than we might realize. This is particularly true in corporate prayer. It is common in prayer meetings for several people to pray for the same things multiple times. Treating the prayer meeting as one long prayer offered through many voices helps keep us on track in this respect. When others pray at prayer meetings, remember that their prayers are your prayers. If you would not, and should not, repeat the same thing over and over again in private prayer, then neither should you repeat what others have prayed in corporate prayer without good reasons for doing so.

There are at least two exceptions to this rule. Repeat a petition when you have something new to add that someone else did not include. However, consider this advice in light of the directions above about not being too specific in public prayer beyond what is necessary. We can also repeat a petition when it represents a peculiar burden on the hearts of those who are present. For example, everyone in the prayer meeting should share a burden for the revival of the church. Concern for the spiritual vitality of the church and the spread of the gospel is virtually a litmus test for a good prayer meeting. Alternatively, a family who has lost a child will weigh heavily on everyone's heart and naturally demand more attention in prayer. Neither God nor man is wearied when such concerns dominate the hearts of those praying.

All of the people in the prayer meeting could, and perhaps should, pray for the revival of the church and the conversion of the world. However, even in these instances we should use a variety of heartfelt and genuine expressions combined with texts of Scripture rather than simply repeating the same requests *ad nauseum*. It is obnoxious when young children sometimes bring the same petitions in virtually the same words to us hoping to wear out our resistance. So we must not treat God as though He is either deaf or unwilling to give better things than we ask of Him in prayer.

This rule does not exclude those who come to God with childlike hearts and who express their prayers through stumbling and broken expressions. Contrary to the self-image of such people, such prayers ascend like incense to heaven and are music to the ears of the saints who pray with them. It is better to pray simply and sincerely than to seek to impress others with our words.

KEEP YOUR PRAYERS BRIEF

It is better for a diverse group of people to offer a few praises and a few petitions each than for a few people to try to pray for everything or to pray for some items in too much detail. If you pray for someone who has cancer, for example, then pray clearly and simply for their spiritual and physical welfare. Others at the meeting do not need to know the results of their current blood tests. Such details rarely affect either the content or the efficacy of our prayers for such people.

Try to avoid praying more than once unless there is some necessity for it. If the group praying is particularly large, then the leadership may need to designate individuals to pray on behalf of everyone. If the prayer meeting is small, then the widest participation possible is desirable. In either case, our prayers should be brief and to the point. Sincere hearts and lively faith, rather than long sentences and expansive vocabularies, are what make the effective fervent prayers of righteous people avail much (James 5:16).

Get to the point quickly in your prayers. Praise God for those attributes that bear most immediately on the content of your prayer. Bring your petitions to Him in light of His character, confessing your sins, and thanking Him for His mercies in Christ's name. As a minister, I was deeply convicted on this point when I realized that one of my elders often prayed for everything that I usually did in public worship, but in less than half the time. God hears us for Christ's sake rather than for the multitude of our words. Let our public prayers be brief.

DO NOT BE A SLAVE TO THE CLOCK

We should neither rush through our prayer meetings with too little time for prayer, nor should we extend our prayer time unduly. If prayer fizzles out early, there is no shame in ending the prayer meeting early. If the Spirit blesses corporate prayer extraordinarily and people are pleading for the spread of the gospel vigorously, do not close the meeting until people have finished. Remember, however, that extraordinary blessings in a prayer meeting must be extraordinary. Otherwise, appealing to the Spirit's alleged blessing can become an excuse to try people's patience. If our prayer meetings are habitually long and tedious because we think that long prayer meetings are a mark of spirituality, we should not be surprised if people stop attending these meetings.

Time will be less of an issue in prayer meetings if most of the time is devoted to prayer rather than to prayer requests or to Bible study. If a study goes too long, then we might feel rushed through our prayers. However, since prayer meetings are ordinarily the only time that we devote to prayer exclusively, we should not shrink from focusing on the business at hand. We should know what time the prayer meeting closes ordinarily. The length of our prayer meetings can be regular in general without making us slaves to the clock in one direction or the other.

DO NOT TURN YOUR PRAYERS INTO SERMONS

Those who pray at prayer meetings speak to God in the presence of others. We must beware that we do not lapse into speaking to people on God's behalf instead. This is one of the worst and most common errors in public prayer. If we say things like, "Lord, we know that you have told us to keep ourselves from temptation and that there are some people here who walk into tempting situations, and that they know they should stop, but they do not, even though I have tried to confront them repeatedly…," then we are preaching rather than praying. Most prayers that begin with, "Lord, we know," run the risk of preaching instead of praying.

Praying in this way comes across as being very similar to the prayer of the Pharisee, who "prayed... with himself" and thanked God that he was not like other men (Luke 18:11). Your goal in prayer should be to express the desires of others through your voice and not to change their opinions and practices through the content of your prayers. If there are issues that should be resolved between church members, or if there are areas where disagreements in doctrine or practice exist, then you should address such things privately.

Church officers need to be particularly cautious in this area. I have seen elders work very hard on their public prayers only for their preparations to backfire. Some habitually quote several stanzas from their favorite hymns. Others cite reputable theologians. I have even heard some quote, explain, and apply large passages of Scripture. While such practices are meant well, they subvert the usefulness and effectiveness of public prayer. Most listeners find these practices obnoxious. Those sitting under such prayers get the impression that they are getting two sermons for the price of one. It is useful for those who lead worship to think through their prayers before praying publicly, but they should always aim to express their hearts to God on behalf of the congregation using clear and direct language and simple expressions.

The simple rule in this regard is to remember that you are addressing God in prayer rather than men. You should address Him in a way that people can understand you and pray with you. Gaining consent is part of the task of corporate prayer; imparting information is not. You should not use expressions in prayer meetings that imply that you are teaching either God or your neighbor something. To speak as though you are informing God in your prayers is foolish, and to seek to impart information to others is inappropriate. People often view those who preach in their prayers as ingenuine, insincere, and self-aggrandizing. You will neither do good to the souls of others nor do any credit to yourself if you turn your prayers into veiled exhortations or expositions of Scripture.

ENCOURAGE ALL TYPES OF PEOPLE TO PRAY

Writing a booklet on how we should pray at prayer meetings implies that we should participate in those meetings by praying. As believers, we should want to pray. Prayer meetings are for the congregation, and congregations should participate in them. In particular, prayer meetings are one of the best opportunities to teach children how to be an active part of the congregation. It is important to bring children to prayer meetings and to teach them how to pray brief prayers. The prayers of children are one of the greatest encouragements to the congregation, and they are one of the best means to foster ownership in children in the task of spreading the gospel. This is often one of the only ways for children to participate in the life and ministry of the church from a young age. This practice also helps prevent children from becoming adults who are content to show up at church once on Sunday, thinking that this is enough to fulfill their membership vows.

The rules that limit and shape our prayers should never discourage the weakest and least informed among us from praying. As with all other things, we learn as we do. We should not avoid participating in prayer because we are afraid that we pray poorly. Prayer meetings are not stages on which contestants compete in performing their most eloquent prayers. They are places in which God's family is gathered and His children express their love for Him and ask Him to help them in their time of need. Though not all Christians should lead public worship or preach or pray there, the prayer meeting is one place in which we should encourage the widest participation possible.

Though this is not the place to settle the controversy and contrary opinions by a church's office-bearers should be respected, it appears that women participated in prayer meetings in Acts 1:14 and other places. Though Paul exhorted the women to be "silent" in public worship (1 Cor. 14:34; 1 Tim. 2:12), they continued in one accord with the apostles and all believers in prayer. On a practical note, sometimes women tend to be more faithful than men in attending prayer meetings. I have led prayer meetings in which I was the only man present. If the women did not pray, this would make for short meetings. I have also led large prayer meetings in which few men were willing to pray. Though I believe that women should participate in prayer meetings, men should also be willing to take leadership in praying. All believers should serve Christ in His church, and they must promote the ministry of the church in a variety of ways. Prayer meetings mark one of the easiest and the best ways of doing so.

REMEMBER IN YOUR PRAYERS TO PRAISE THE TRIUNE GOD

The Westminster Shorter Catechism closes appropriately by reminding us that in our prayers we should praise God (Q. 107). If our petitions in our prayer meetings overshadow our praises, then we should remind ourselves of the biblical model for prayer. We should praise the triune God for who He is and for what He has done. We pray to the Father in Christ's name through and for the Holy Spirit. In prayer, we actively engage in worshiping and depending on all three persons in the Trinity.

This last point brings us to where we began in this booklet. We should pray for our needs and for those of others in light of the first three petitions of the Lord's Prayer. All of our petitions should promote God's glory and His reputation in the world, through us and through others. Though prayer is many things, it is an act of worship above all else. Use prayer meetings as occasions to worship and glorify the Lord together.

It is better to praise God with united hearts and voices than to do so alone (look at the Psalms for numerous examples of this!). Praising God and seeking His glory in corporate prayer is one of the best ways to advance Christ's kingdom and to edify the church. I have never heard a Christian say that there was too much worship and thanksgiving at a prayer meeting. This is what we will be doing when all the saints and angels are gathered in glory at the Last Day, and we see Christ face to face. Do not forget to praise Him in your corporate prayers.